1

Back On Track

ISBN 978-1-915787-32-3

Printed by
Biddles Books
Kings Lynn
Norfolk
PE32 1SF

Back On Track

Introduction ...

Welcome to this, my fourth full collection of poems,
songs, prose – call it what you will.
The title refers not only to the freedom from covid
restrictions , but also to getting out of a rut
and to where I want to be.
Again in this collection I have mixed many styles of
poetic form.
This collection was all written between 2020 and 2022
with the exception of **'The man—the legend'** which I
wrote in 1980 having heard of the tragic death of John
Lennon.
Hope you find something that you like

Photo credits
Front cover - Michele Richardson
Back cover and page 169 - Janet Rubanik
Page 7 - Georgia Leigh Taylor
Page 193 - Kim Ashworth
Drawings - SPT

Back On Track

The fourth collection of poems by

Steven P. Taylor

Steven P. Taylor

Life for everyone has been changed since the Covid lockdowns. Personally, my life went in all sorts of directions with work, health and also, sadly, I lost my mother in Nov 2021.

My poetry however, has been going from strength to strength. My live work has become so varied, from doing Women's Institute lunchtime talks to supporting rock bands in theatres, working on the poetry scene and doing my own sell out, theatre shows, which were a great thrill. I have met a lot of interesting and influential people during this time and constantly look forward to what comes next.

The live work is so important to me as it helps me gauge the quality of the material before committing it to print.

If you should wish to book me for any type of show or a commission, please get in touch through the contacts below

Web ...www.stevenptaylorpoetry.com
Email ... stevetaylorok@aol.com
Tel 07764573483
https://www.facebook.com/steve.taylor.39/
https://www.instagram.com/spt.poet_/
Twitter... @steveok

'Are there enough mirrors for you sir?'

Bury Met 24th February 2022 - pre show

CONTENTS

CONTENTS

DRAWN TOGETHER

Our relationship on paper
Was sketchy but fine
We were drawn together
By an artist friend of mine

BACK ON TRACK

I've been to places
Felt madness traces
Where fear embraces
Distorted faces

I've seen the sights
The flashing lights
The pointless fights
The sleepless nights

I've persevered
Through floods of tears
And constant fears
What seemed like years

But I'm back
Yes I'm back on track

I've witnessed things
That this life brings
Heard tuneless strings
Felt broken wings

Seen families trying
As children crying
While Politicians' lying
The good are dying

The silenced voice
That makes no noise
That has no choice
As sound destroys

But I'm back
Yes I'm back on track

Deals on the table
Without a label
From minds unstable
And bodies unable

Fate is decreed
As wounded bleed
As healers plead
Desperation and need

Now the things in my mind
The doctrines that bind
The freedoms declined
Will forever remind

But I'm back
Yes I'm back on track

And I hope and I pray
This low road highway
That drives all away
Will give me my day

Where that mind place, so dark
Reality disembarked
And the only remark
Was the black dogs bark

Those that were leaving
Thought under achieving
Actions disbelieving
Seeing is bereaving

But I'm back
Yes I'm back
Thank god
I'm back on track

I PLAY WITH PROSE

I live in literature
I languish in language
I substitute standards
I slip into slanguage
I work with words
I tangle with tones
I wrangle with rhymes
Bring the beef to the bones
I mutter with meter
I struggle with stanza
I study in sentence
To bring a bonanza
I negotiate the noun
I negate the norm
I facilitate the flow
I fracture the form
I fumble and flourish
In fictitious foreplay
I forge a fantasy
Founded on fair play
I frolic with phrases
I fiddle with feelings
I model the moral
I meddle with meanings
I proffer profanities
I produce paragraphs

I let loose in lyric
I linger for laughs
I tumble with type
I toy with terminology
I expound exclamation
I entertain etymology
I vocalise vision
I venture in verse
I compile by conjunction
I craft and I curse
I create with the content
I confide in the caper
I ponder and pause
To put poems on the paper

ATHENA GIRL

Adolescent years, girl from Athena
Filling my thoughts in my fantasy arena

More than just an image on a wall in a frame
To this keen teenager tennis was the game

Taken my mind, serving from above
Taken my heart, fifteen love

If the worlds my oyster she was the pearl
A proper nineteen seventies, cheeky girl

Feelings up and down like a roller coaster
Adorn a bedroom wall, my girl on the poster

Circle my north star my own Ursa Major
Knowing who you are, advantage teenager

Decorate the room, illuminate the mind
Self satisfaction, this way love is blind

Giving me a dream, make me out a menace
Is it really wrong to have a new found love for tennis

In my own little world, this my perfect catch
Teenage love story, game, set and match

FUTURE AND FATE

Twenty twenty two
A world I thought I knew
Yet discrimination is rife
How can man be taught
To not give a thought
To equality in life

And the place to begin
With colour of skin
Is to always be equally treated
No one's born to be hateful
We're all born and grateful
And racism can be defeated

When they fought with bravery
To abolish slavery
And make every human the same
Yet still to this day
They are treated this way
And we stand and we shirk from the blame

Our future and our fate
Is teach love and not hate
And embrace every race as one
And it's only whenever
We all come together
We truly can say that we've won.

HEARTBURN

To facilitate my acid reflux control
Every day I take Omeprazole
This here prescription seems the best
To stop that burning in the chest
And if the buggers still not gone
Then next up is the Nexium
All these things bring discomfort cessation
'I'm just talking 'bout my medication'

It's hard to live with acid reflux
A burning throat that really sucks
The fuss that all this is creating
My eating habits debilitating
I feel like I'm really an incomplete man
Till I've taken a dose of Buscupan
I've got to have my acid sedation
'Just talking 'bout my medication'

There's no easy way to fully appease
Gastro oesophageal reflux disease
And if the condition continues then is
The time to dig out the trusty Rennies
How best to make the situation placid
And banish that bloody excessive acid
These drugs are my god sent salvation
'Just talking 'bout my medication'

How can I really have a good time?
If I can't have pies and chips and wine
And chocolate that's another one
That sends me for the Gaviscon
This stomach problem has me beat
When all I want to do is eat
Instead I must take chalk libation
'Just talking 'bout my medication
My medication'

THE 23T BUS

The 23T bus to Bolton
I'll paint a little vignette
Of that classic bus route
I never will forget
Bury through to Bolton
Was the journey brief
Kay gardens through Breightmet
To New Zealand Chief
The Navada disco was waiting
The place was all the rage
For a gang of eager teenagers
Lying about their age
The 23T to Bolton
The conveyance to rely on
The secret to enlightenment
The passage into Zion
Ascend the curving stairway
Take the upper seats
Check hair in the mirror on route
Looking pretty neat
The after shave aroma
A splash of Brut 33
Hi Karate and Old Spice
In the air on the 23T

On the 23T to Bolton
With a players cigarette
A vacant place on the back row
With the girls; the scene is set
The 23T to Bolton
Where anyone who's anyone meet
Take us to a better place
Take us to easy street
Set to walk the walk
Parade your finest gear
The weekend comes alive
The atmosphere starts here
The 23T to Bolton
It's running till after 11
Taking us out of the mundane
To Navada, nirvana, heaven
Transportation to teenage dreams
It's the only place to be
We wouldn't learn the ways of the world
Without the 23T
It's where you get your education
I'm quite certain you can see
You ain't lived if you ain't had a snog
On the back seat of the 23T

VOCABLES

Vocables, vocables
They are in all the songs
Vocables, vocables
Come on sing along

Bum bumty bum bum
La la la
Dick a dick a dum dum
Da da da

Vocables, vocables
Sing some too
Do wah diddy diddy
Dum diddy do

Ying tong ying tong
Boom bang a bang
Ding dong ding dong
Shang, shang a Lang

Vocables, vocables
Just you and me
Sha la la sha la la
Sha la la la lee

Bom bom bom
ba bom ba bom bom
Da da da
Da do Ron Ron

Vocables, vocables
Bomp de Bomp de bomp
Dip de dip de dip
Rama lama ding dong

Da doo doo doo
Da da da da
Be bob a Lula
Ob la di ob la da

Vocables, vocables
Now we're in the mood
Na na na / na na na na /
na na na na hey Jude

(keep repeating till all leave)

SO THAT WAS CHRISTMAS

Turkey roasted
Pigs in blankets
Gifts of scarves
Socks and hankies
Christmas jumpers
Paper hats
Get togethers
Chats and spats
Relatives round
Family meeting
Excess drinking
Over eating
Christmas dinner
Spend the cash
Carrots, cabbage
Roast and mash
Swede and parsnips
Stuffing, peas
Sprouts and
Cauliflower cheese
Twiglets, cashews
Figs and dates
Things you never
Ever ate

On the TV
Charlie's speech
With a little
Drinky each
TV specials
Anticipating
Was it really
Worth the waiting
Friends arriving
Friends departing
Grandpa snoring
Burping farting
Mince pies puddings
Apple crumble
Party music
Late night fumble
Drink starts talking
Head is empty
In the morning
Regrets a plenty
Pointless presents
Polar postmark
Party poppers
Pants from Primark
Paris perfume
Potpourri
Plastic Partridge
Plastic pear-tree

THE ROUX BROTHERS

I went for the dining of Michel Roux
Of the famous cooking Roux brothers
La Gavroche with three Michelin stars
Was a class ahead of the others

People said you should try the food
Of his brother Albert Roux
Albert ran the Waterside Inn
So I thought I'd give it a do

The restaurant was also three Michelin stars
So I went and I took my mother
We didn't enjoy the food, which just shows
You can't judge a cook by his brother

AGEING AIN'T EASY

Ageing ain't easy
It comes with diseases
With aches and pains
And toilet strains
Weakening brains
And varicose veins
Constant sweating
Worrying, forgetting
Doctor's appointments
Rubbing ointments
Taking pills
To ward off ills
Transplants
Big pants
Wrinkles, liver spots
Shingles, chamber pots
Heavy frown
When sitting down
Fewer smiles
With painful piles
Feeling regretful
Panicky, fretful
Hearing aids, glasses
No luck with the lassies
No hair on your head
Ears and noses instead
You've withering parts
Involuntary farts

Burning hot flushes
Quick toilet rushes
Ailments battling
Tablets rattling
Sagging and drooping
Hunching and stooping
Surgical stockings
Looking quite shocking
Rheumatoid arthritis
Asthma and bronchitis
Your expected vanity
Drives you to insanity
Your joints are worn
And you look forlorn
Bones clicking and creaking
And parts of you leaking
You feel doom and gloom
As you walk in a room
And you suddenly sigh ......
When you can't remember why
Your water works don't
Your certain urges wont
You're right up the junction
With erectile disfunction
Things won't harden
In your grey front garden
Oh you feel uneasy
And slightly queasy
Coughing and wheezy
Yeh ageing ain't easy

THE ROCKER AT THE OPEN MIC

He walks into the bar
With his carefully crafted look
Like a caricature rock star
In a fantasy comic book
His reflective silver shades
Reflecting his lack of taste
His studded leather belt
Straining round his waist
His tatty denim waistcoat
And greying hairy back
His look is made complete
With a spread of builders crack
He walks across the room
Guitar in his hand
His face a shade of tango
From a bottle of fake tan
He wears his jeans too tight
Drinks too many beers
Hasn't seen his little lad
In many, many years
But all this doesn't stop him
Getting on the stage
A walking anachronism
From a bygone age
He gets a set reaction
From all there in the room
As he sings as only he can
Mostly out of tune

He doesn't see the funny side
His sense of humour is crushed
He goes on quite oblivious
Masked by his ego rush
Wears flashy snake skin shoes
And a leather cowboy hat
He thinks he looks the part
I think he looks a twat
He lives in his own little world
The poor deluded chap
A modern day Walter Mitty
A one man Spinal Tap
He blasts out his rockin tunes
Laced with booming bass
His sweat is black with hair dye
Running down his face
He can't hold an audience
He can't even hold a tune
He's cashing in his rock n roll chips
At the last chance saloon
The bar has started closing
The clock has struck eleven
He bids farewell in time honoured style
Murdering stairway to heaven
If he did this for a living
His future would be bleak
But despite his ability his ego says
He'll be back again next week

TOGETHER

Gonna start a band
Me and you
We'll tour the land
And see it through
From Chinatown
To Timbuktu
We'll play around
We'll sing the blues
No one tells us
What to do
There'll be no fuss
Just me and you

Gonna have some fun
You and me
Let the engine run
We're breaking free
Take our load
We're gonna see
Hit that road
Just let it be
We'll spend our time
Writing poetry
And drinking wine
Just you and me

So here we go
It's now us two
And we will show
We'll stick like glue
Will rock the place
It's what we do
Embrace the bass
And see it through
Our future planned
The dream is true
We named our band
It's 'me and you'

A few different poetry styles

Limerick
The classic five line poem and probably the first type of structured poetry that most people try, usually written as comic poems, often rude and there's no place for that in this book !

Haiku
Haiku is an ancient form of Japanese poetry containing 17 syllables shared between three lines that are arranged in a pattern of 5-7-5. I'm not a big fan of this poetic form, although I love one by the guvner 'John Cooper Clarke'

'To freeze the moment
In seventeen syllables
Is very diffic'

Villanelle
This is possibly my favourite style of writing, as it's a very challenging and somewhat confusing format to write.
I think of it like a jigsaw puzzle
It's a French poetry style with a curious rhyming pattern, structure and repetition.
I have found that villanelle poems work well as songs. This first one here was written about the character 'Villanelle' from the novels and TV series 'Killing Eve.'

Cyrch a chwta
This is a welsh form of poetry formed in 8 line stanza with 7 syllables per line. All lines have the same end rhyme except line 7 which rhymes in the centre.
All straightforward enough eh?

I'm not going to attempt to explain the structure of the villanelle or my head will explode.

VILLANELLE (a villanelle)

A changing face with changing mother tongue
Insidiously plays the deadly game
At any cost will right another wrong

So tunefully she sings her special song
And nothing now will ever be the same
That changing face and changing mother tongue

Dispatches in her own stylistic way
Then distanced from the cause and from the blame
At any cost will right another wrong

Then infiltrates the darkened close of day
Can't blow away that never ending flame
Of changing face and changing mother tongue

They say it's all for love and not for pay
But when the job is given that's the aim
At any cost will right another wrong

And when she's on the eve she does belong
No further need to linger or to stay
A changing face a changing mother tongue
At any cost will right another wrong.

DOORS (a villanelle)

The doors that lead to a future for you
Opportunities lie there for the take
The doors are open for you to go through

Leading to the goals that you will pursue
Routes that you select, decisions you make
The doors that lead to a future for you

Look down the track and see the way you turned
The time was propitious to make the break
The doors are open for you to go through

If only for the chance that you had yearned
And all that in your past you did forsake
The doors that lead to a future for you

Take the chances through advances you have learned
And know the odds before you set the stake
The doors are open for you to go through

Take on the challenge and take in the view
Take the doors for which you now are concerned
The doors that lead to a future for you
The doors are open for you to go through

LIMERICKS

A friend of mine called Moriarty
Was in demand to speak at a party
He'd recite Keats and Wilde
And drink halves of mild
But I found him too arty farty

Poetry's got into a rut
The doors to rudeness are shut
To get notoriety
It needs more variety
And plenty of nob gags and smut

My friend had quite a to do
When he had his first vindaloo
Was the hottest one known
And on the way home
He farted and followed through

THE NIGHT SHIFT (a Cyrch a chwta)

Her time would chime with delight
Victimless crime in red light
Yet she, a slave to her plight
Could see and brave without fright
And crave for flames to ignite
Under seducing moonlight
Wonder producing with ease
Falls to knees to please this night

HAIKU

I don't understand
How Haiku poems work so
I'll give them a miss

Most Haiku you find
If you're looking for a time
Doesn't often rhyme

Just five syllables
Followed then by seven more
Haiku is a bore

TIME TO GO (June 2022)

When the trust has gone forever
When the battle can't be won
When support has all but dropped
When unity has gone

When the signs are everywhere
When the writings on the wall
When criticism is unending
It's time to listen to the call

When there is no solidarity
The party irreparably split
When you're hanging by your ego
You know it's time to quit

When your work mates have no confidence
When your public's saying no
When your friends talk behind your back
Surely it's time to go

THE BOY IN THE CORNER

The boy in the corner is thinking
As he re-sticks the tape on his glasses
What will he hear what will he feel
As he makes his way to his classes

Maybe they'll push or trip him
Laugh at the hole in his shoes
They are ever more creative
In the ways of abuse that they use

The boy in the corner is staring
At the lunch box he brought in today
No chocolate bar or cheddars
The other boys took them away

And what did he ever do wrong
To deserve to be treated this way
Is the question he can't seem to answer
So it still carries on everyday

The boy in the corner is crying
But there's no place in this class for tears
And the sympathy is non existent
Just a barrage of laughter and jeers

And sitting at home on his own now
The thoughts of school are haunting
Endlessly running the gauntlet
The quips the jokes and the taunting

The boy in the corner says 'mummy
I just don't know where to start
But thank you for always being here
I love you with all my heart'

And finally he finds the answer
To make all of this go away
Now the bullies must look for another
There's no boy in the corner today

The boy in the corner is peaceful ......

HE'S AT THE GYM

He's a body builder
He's a muscle fanatic
He's got a gymnasium
Up in his attic

He's in the gym for hours
Doing his stuff
Pumping on the iron,
Gotta get buff

Gotta get buff
Gotta get tough
These smokin guns
Are never big enough

Get that rippling body
As perfect as you can
Top it all off with
A spray of fake tan

Always check the mirror
Me, me, me, me, me
Now the all important bit
Let everybody see

Gotta get buff
Gotta get tough
These smokin guns
Are never big enough

So wear a skimpy t-shirt
Wear a little vest
Show us all your muscles
Show us all the rest

Bronzy bulging biceps
Pulsating preening pecs
Manley mountain muscles
But sod all in his kecks

Gotta get buff
Gotta get tough
These smokin guns
Are never big enough

Oppressive obsessive
Egotistic
Compelling compulsive
Narcissistic

He's gotta get that physique
Looking pretty sick
....Or he could get a life
The self obsessed prick.

WITHOUT YOU

A day in early springtime
A gentle morning breeze
A walk along the avenue
By swaying stooping trees
I see the sun is shining
In a sky of perfect blue
It may as well be black and white
In a world that's without you

A cacophony of sound
Of children all at play
Innocence and laughter
An affable affray
And the children in their minds
Have a million things to do
I can't think of a single one
In a world that's without you

Time we spent outside
On the garden with the flowers
Planting seeds and tending
Spending many hours
But I don't have a reason
To watch seedlings coming through
If I can't share the beauty
In a world that's without you

There's so much going on
That I'll try to embrace
And I'll look to the future
With the memory of your face
But I know when I look back
When it was just we two
It will never be the same
In a world that's without you

COUNT

Count the months
Count the years
Count the heartache
Count the tears

Count the celebrations
Count the birthdays
Easter, Christmas
Summer holidays
Out for long walks
Weekends away
Having long talks
Away for the day

Count the days
Count the weeks
Count the highs
Count the peaks

Session at the local
A sing along time
A chance to be vocal
It's no great crime
Watching a film
A night at the flix
So many ways
To get our kicks

Count the minutes
Count the hours
Count on love
We said was ours

Count the promises
Broken in two
Count the times
It was not me and you
Count the lies
Count the deceit
All the betrayal
Low down cheat

Count the seconds
Ticking away
Hear the whistle
For close of play
Count the transgressions
In your head
Count the visitors
In your bed
Count the times
You look at your phone
And hope for release
From being alone

Count yourselves lucky
You'd someone who shared
Count yourself lucky
You'd someone who cared
Count the good friends
On the way that you lost
Add it all up
And now count the cost

THE ARTIST

Using colours as his words
Strokes as his emotions
Dreams flowed from the palette
In primary mixed potions

Images emerge in shades
Tones and moods and feelings
Swept surely crossing canvas
With relevance and meaning

A hidden personality
Within the style and grace
Exhibited in humility
Trapped in the artists face

Catching changing seasons
January to December
All year long legacy
Within the art remembered

THE DYING SWAN

I was sitting on the floor in a darkened place
And through the thick smoke I saw Vivienne's face
She beckoned and smiled with those come to dread eyes
And predictably then to no one's surprise
I crossed the room slowly and sat by her side
There were never refusals however I tried
And together again we went off to our world
To look and to learn as our futures unfurled
We started our journey to lands never dreamed
Of tranquil beauty of wishes redeemed
And the clouds darted by at the speed of thought
And the world wasn't looking the way we were taught
As the birds descended to break up the calm
And the pretty ballerina performed with such charm
The hands on the clock were pointing at three
And the hands in the room were pointing at me
And I froze to the spot at the dancers face
As Vivienne now had taken her place
And the pace wasn't steady as slowly she moved
And I called out to say she had nothing to prove
And I wanted to help to stop her from falling
But softly I heard distant voices were calling
And I heard my name mentioned and mentioned again
I could not take in this monotonous refrain

Still I watched and I smiled and felt prouder and prouder
As the voices around came closer and louder
And the clouds burst apart and a life storm took hold
Her frail body shook, her hand icy cold
As uniformed figures appeared all around
Staring at me helpless there on the ground
Lifeless and silent aware yet afraid
As the journey concludes and light starts to fade
And my Vivienne's voice echo's round in my head
And I think of all of the things left unsaid
And I wished and I prayed to relive this last day
As my sweet ballerina drifted away.

THE JAZZ SINGER

In a quiet, smoky, dim lit cellar
The magic of a cool jazz mix
A voice that could be Dinah or Ella
Has all in the room transfixed

The pleasure today to sing and play
And it's all about the song
But there's more to it than that
When the baggage comes along

As an unrelenting media
Are hounding to spoil the game
And the simple joy of singing now
Can never be the same

All around pile endless pressure
A release is needed from that
And the love that is thrilling is killing
And the love is the man in the hat

In her world of insecurity
Flying too high so to crack
A life of manipulation
A life turning back to black

Learning the bi product is fame
A solitary figure in need
With parasitical paparazzi
Watching their victim bleed

Standing alone in a spotlight
Standing alone in a life
Driven through hell by the media
Cutting through life like a knife

And the cries for help go unheard
As all want a piece of her now
And the media show no compassion
There's no conscience there anyhow

The darkness came over so often
Clouds that gathered too much
Lost love left her feeling forgotten
Not even a warm hand to touch

And how it could have been so different
For memories are all that she has
When all she ever wanted from life
Was to bring her thing to sing jazz

That voice that kept on shining through
Will shine on still everyday
Will the press think twice and learn now
.... As fame takes another away

LIFE IS....

Life's a job for two
Whatever it is you do
It's better with two

Life's a thing to share
A time to show you care
It's best to share

Life's too short to waste
Savour every taste
Let no time waste

Life's a precious gift
Don't just let it drift
Use that precious gift

Life's an opportunity
To live together in unity
Take that opportunity

Life is for living
For loving and giving
Do some real living

Life's for learning
Earning and yearning
Keep on learning

Life is to travel
To see things unravel
See that you travel

Life is for love
So give and take love
Make lots of love

WHATEVER HAPPENED TO PETER?

Whatever happened to Peter
He seem to peter away
Then there's Noel, Nigel and Neville
You don't hear of them today

There are no Donalds and Ronalds
No one calls their son Kevin or Dave
You hardly ever see a Lee
Will these names ever be saved

Would you want your daughter to marry a Gary
Would she stick with a Mick or a Nick or a Rick
How about Bernard or Brian or Barry
Or maybe she just prefers Dick

So search through all the lists
Looking for a good name for men
It wouldn't be Douglas or Gordon
Nor would it be Glen, Ben or Ken

Tell me who,
Would wannabe Stu
We're not seein an Ian,
There's no calling for a Colin
You're never gonna miss,
A Jim or a Chris

No one names a boy,
Trevor, John or Roy
There are no calls,
For Phils or Pauls
No feel for a Neil
And avoid Tim and Craig,
Like the bubonic plague
Franks drawn a blank
And we're not avin any Gavin
Wayne is on the wane
You'll never get a heart throb
.... called Bob

So now they're all Jacob and Oscar and Leo
Why they use these names is a mystery
So get used to Archie and Levi and Theo
As all the best names are consigned to history
Even
Steven

HERE I LIVE

It's not just a greenbelt fighting adversity
But a living community of great diversity

'I live on the grass, I run through the field
We live here en masse, the field is our shield
I fly and collect twigs and nest in the tree
And the tree is my shelter, the safe place for me
I skip between branches, the tree stores my food
Make home for my young, protecting my brood
I look after all that I choose to create,
And the plants and the flowers that I pollinate.'

But then come the diggers on council instruction
To rip up this beauty and turn to destruction

'You take away my trees, my branches and my nest
You take away all these, I have no place to rest
You take away my home, the hedges and the woods
I've nowhere now to roam, life doesn't look too good
You take away my ponds, the rain pools and the streams
All the vegetation, nothing matters now it seems
You take away my food, this way I can't survive
It's gone away for good, no way to stay alive
You desecrate environment with not a thought for cost
What was a thriving part of nature, now forever lost
So replace it all now, with your trucks of concrete load
And one day you will find me, lying dead beside the road'.

SUCH A NIGHT

I wake up in your room to the breaking light
As I gaze in awe at such a wondrous sight
A gap in the curtains throws a ray that ends night
Such a night

Your hair that cascades over shoulders so bare
And I look at the beauty and try not to stare
And if I believed, I'd say magic lies there
Such a care

And the silk sheets absorb your porcelain skin
And wrap up the sight that put me in a spin
And to say how I feel, there's no place to begin
Such a sin

There's a look that I can't quite define now as such
But it's something that I care about very much
And it starts in your eyes and runs through your touch
Such a touch

You can't say that it's love, yet it feels just the same
Excuses and reasons are all pretty lame
But it's handling blame that's the name of the game
Such a shame

PARIS

Drive me through Paris
Drink some champagne
Take me to the river
Let's go in Seine

Streets are breezy
Some parts sleazy
Take life easy
On the Champs-Elysees

Time now to spend
Time now to move
No time to lose
Toulouse in the Louvre

Watch the lady stare
Walk a gallery mile
Charismatic sigh
Enigmatic smile

See the Arc de Triomphe and
Place de la Concorde
Sights to behold here
Oui d'accord

Sacre Coeur
The sacred heart
Basilica beats
The heart of Montmartre

Our Lady of Paris
Imperiously pretty
Notre Dame reigns
The Ile e la Cite

Grotesques of Pont Neuf
Like Hugo's creation
And miserable sorts
Are lost in translation

The city of light
La Ville Lumiere
Art and gastronomy
Filling the air

A final encounter
One thousand feet high
La dame de fer
That pierces the sky

Get an eyeful of the power
At the Champ de Mars
Of Gustave's tower
Then say au revoir

SHARING

Sharing this moment with you tonight
Sharing this moment with you
Sharing this moment with
Sharing this moment
Sharing this
Sharing
Shhh

MORE

I want to do new things more
Enjoy what life brings more
Take on different tasks more
When I need help, ask more
And when I have worries I'll talk more
Attempt to get fitter and walk more
Could even maybe run more
Go out more and have fun more
With my friends I'll share more
Be there more and care more
Let things be spoken more
I'll vow to be open more
Give up my time more
Look to prosper and shine more
Create and cultivate more
Innovate and appreciate more
Help others and give more
Have lovers and live more
In all try to see more
In myself try to be more
Let go and be free more
And if trying harder is
The solution
That's my New Year's
Resolution

GOODBYE (MR.) POTATO HEAD *(written after the announcement that the Mr' was to be dropped)*

I'm gonna miss the Mister, of Mister potato head
Now without the Mister is the way it must be said
Gender specific terms will all be banned
'Mr and Mrs' will just become 'and'
Everything we now know will worsen
The Isle of Man will be the Isle of Person
Why a mister will no longer be
Is a mister mystery to me
What I know for sure is this
I will certainly miss a Mrs or Miss
The way it's going , then very soon
They're going to evict the Man in the moon.
No more stingy Mr Mean
They're going to polish off Mr Sheen
Everyone going again and again
The Mr Men won't be Mr or Men
The whole things getting awfully confusing
I don't know the terminology to be using

We must ignore
Signor
Mustn't infer
Monsieur
Lad and lass
We must bypass

Girl and boy
Will annoy
Guy and fella
Come under same umbrella
To say sir
Or him or her
Is to err
Using Madam
Another bad un
Saying chap
May bring a slap
The term, bloke
Is no joke
And the band Mr. Mister
Will be history

So.....
No more Mr. Know it all
No more Mr Blue sky
No more Mr Muscle
No more Mr. Nice guy

No more Lady luck
That would cause offense
Goodbye Mr. Chips
Goodbye common sense

MORNING WALK

It's getting grim
It's getting rough
I'm piss wet through
I've had enough
I'm in the dark
I'm in the rain
I'm in a gale
I feel the pain
It's pounding down
My clothes are drenched
I'm in the freezing
Cold entrenched
I'm in a state
I'm all alone
I'm many miles
Away from home
I feel so weak
My strength has gone
Can barely move
I can't go on
But wait, I feel
You've been misled
It was a dream
I'm still in bed

THE ROAD OF LOVE

The road of love is a cul de sac
The journey of romance a dead end
The route I take to get near to you
Directs me round the bend

I'm going the wrong way on a one way street
Along the highway of gloom
There are no U-turns to facilitate our meet
Allowed on the motorway of doom

I programmed the Sat Nav to happiness
By the easiest route to take
The one that went via true love
The one that avoided heartbreak

I set the direction that I'm sure of
But turn up a no through road
Would try a detour if I could
But all lanes to your heart run cold

There's no point going on now
This bad road can't be mended
The pot holes of my journey mean
My car crash love has ended

QUEUE

We queue for the taxi
We queue for the bus
We do it politely
Without any fuss

It's a modern phenomenon
A sign of our times
This odd compulsion
To stand up in lines

We queue in the shops
The banks and the bars
We queue on the M62
In our cars

We stand there politely
In order and quietly
Any queue jumpers are
Outcasts of society

We queue at the airport
At passport control
We grump and we tut
It's the way that we roll

We queue for the toilet
We're desperate to do
We queue for the cafe
And we queue for a brew

And throughout our life
Whatever we're doing
I'll tell you for sure
We spend most of it queuing.

And when we leave this world
Whatever be our fate
You can bet there'll be a queue
At heavens pearly gates

ISLAND OF BEAUTY

The sun sets over
The crystal waters
Its reflection forming
A shimmering path
From the horizon.
Across the bay
Black silhouetted mountains
Loom imperiously over the water.
The whitewashed houses
Adorned with bougainvillea
Dotted across
The surrounding hills,
Gaze down on the opulence
Of the tranquil harbour.
Fishermen's boats juxtapose
With majestic yachts
In the shallow bay,
Lightly bobbing on the tide.
As the bar lights flicker
In the moving water
A warm gentle breeze
Causes palms to
Sway in rhythm.
Deserted beaches

Guarded by long shadows
Of redundant parasols.
Smells and sounds
Unique to this place
Hypnotise the senses
And set the mood.
The scent of the lemon trees
Fill the air with
A light, crisp citrus aroma.
In the trees the cicadas
Play their familiar timbal tunes.
A lone gull circles hopefully
At the lapping water's edge.
A waft of fresh seafood
Being prepared at the
Restaurants on the bay
Tempts both potential customers
And expectant seabirds.
Cats wander barely noticed
Under tables of garrulous diners.
A distant Spanish guitar
Plays romantically
Setting the perfect soundtrack
To this idyllic setting.
On my Mediterranean
Island of beauty.

KILLING TIME

Why kill time
Why not use time
Productively
Do things with time
That you will enjoy
Some you may regret
But you can use time
To reflect and learn
There isn't enough time
So pack it tightly
Count time in seconds
Not years
Use every minute wisely
Time is so precious
That bit between
Birth and death
Why kill time
Time is life
Life is short
Too short
If it's not nurtured
And savoured
And appreciated
And used well
It'll fly by

With things left undone
Things left unsaid
Why kill time
And have regrets
Of what you could have done
Because before you know it
The best time has gone
It went by
While you were killing time
Why kill time
It's an endangered species
It may become extinct

THE NEW WAY
(written after I held a door open for someone only to be then told 'I can open doors myself')!

I've respect for a person's identity
And how they may want to be known
I have no issue with lifestyles and choice
And one's life to embrace and to own

But all isn't such plain sailing these days
It isn't just live and let live
There's ambiguity and confusion
There's lots more take than give

Be careful to not put your foot in it
Don't wanna be some kind of scaremonger
But they used to say mind your P's and Q's
Now the P's and Q's are getting longer

I'm wary to open and hold a door
Or to give up my seat on a bus
To help the elderly or infirm
For fear of starting a fuss

Being polite and considerate it seems
Will probably cause a row
Don't show old fashioned courteousness
It's not done to be chivalrous now

And what were once terms of endearment
Are now considered a slur
I understand not saying love or dear
But we now avoid him and her

It's put down to awareness of choice
But brings with it division and sadness
How affection and friendliness causes offence
It's twenty first century madness

HIDDEN IN VIEW

Maybe an enigma
A mystery
To solve
A swirling stigma
From history
Revolves

A new yesterday
From a time
That has been
Or a part in a play
Like a line
In a scene

But still ever changing
Character
Traits
Inside rearranging
The actor
Waits

Unwilling to show
Exhibit
Lay bare
Unable to grow
Prohibits
A care

One dimensional
With a speech
Unheard
Thoughts unintentional
That can't reach
The word

Last scene to steal
Will improve
The task
And the slow reveal
To remove
The mask

I LIVE MY LIFE ON SOCIAL MEDIA

I live my life on social media
My every single move is on the net
I bare myself naked to all each day
In a communication mindset

I post details of my exercises
So everyone knows I'm getting thinner
I post pictures of the walks that I do
Then pictures of my fish and chip dinner

I live my life on social media
Twenty four hours a day I'm active
Using filters on pictures on 'Snapchat'
To try and make me look more attractive

I comment on all the posts that I see
On Instagram, Facebook and Twitter
I comment that I'm having a great day
When really I'm having a shitter

I live my life on social media
It's the way that I show how I care
I join in discussions and arguments
I 'like,' I 'retweet,' and I 'share'

I've boarded the broadcasting bandwagon
It seems it's what everyone does
Posting homemade video clips online
And getting the 'you tube' buzz

I live my life on social media
All the time getting excited
Thinking back to the good old days
Of 'my space' and 'friends reunited'

Use LinkedIn, What'sApp and Tumbler
Messenger and Pinterest
Soundcloud, We Chat and Tik Tok
For all social media interest

I live my life on social media
To the exclusion of all others
Leave me alone with a laptop
The internet's my live in lover

I don't need a fancy education
I've learnt all I know from Wikipedia
I'm happy in my virtual world
I live my life on social media

BREAKFAST BOOZIN'

I wander the streets in a morning rut
I've been up since before half past seven
No place for a drink, the pubs are all shut
Nowhere opens till after eleven

Then along comes the drinker's saviour
An entrepreneur called Tim Martin
With his range of pubs known as Wetherspoons
Now this will be sure to enhearten

This is no Savoy or place to fine dine
It's certainly not any Tiffany's
But what it is, is it's open at 9
Welcome to 'Breakfast at Timothy's'

So you want an early morning reckie
A hair of the dog to cure all
Or a pint and a full English brekky
Then this is your first port of call

It's open when all else are sleeping
Just you and the milkman about
Serving for 15 hours a day
At spoons you'll not go without

The beers are flowing all the way
The name of the game is consistency
The hops are the first of your five a day
When you partake in 'Breakfast at Timothy's'

There are meals being served up all day
Despatched with almost a smile
There are distant toilet facilities
In a walk of less than a mile

They attract an eclectic cross section
A little of all humankind
If you're studying evolution
Spoons is a wonderful find

Whether yours is bitter, lager or stout
Its supplying refreshments sufficiently
Whether upwardly mobile or down and out
The day starts with 'Breakfast at Timothy's'

Low prices are Wetherspoons wherewithal
It's the cheapest beer in the vicinity
So if for no other reason at all
A good argument for 'Breakfast at Timothy's'

CHRISTMAS TIME

Is a special time
A precious time
It's a family time
A fantasy time
A cheery time
A beery time
It's a loving time
A do nothing time
A meeting time
Drink and eating time
It's a giving time
A forgiving time
A thoughtful time
A thankful time
A celebratory time
Communicatory time
A rejoicing time
Happy voicing time
A remembering time
Assembling time
A hearty time
A party time
A glistening time
A listening time

A reflecting time
A protecting time
A caring time
A sharing time
A homely time
… a lonely time

THE MAN — A LEGEND

The man - a legend
Much more than a man
A talent, creator
From nothing began
Art school student
Ideas of a sound
A meeting, a friendship
More friends from around.
The birth of an era
From Caverns dark walls
To Hamburg with silver
The Stars mighty halls
A registered marriage
To work and to love
A debut recording
In St. John's Wood
Sixty four on the road
And news of a son
USA and a book
And honours are won
A film, a revolver
Unfinished painting
Japanese lady
To make an acquaintance

The death of a manager
Lonely hearts in
The magical tour
It's a mystery within
A steady romance
Ends the marriage of love
And so Let it be
From Apple above
A ballad, a tribute
But close to the end
A comeback, Toronto
And damages mend
Political protests
Peace that is yearned
Through starving Biafra
The honours returned
The death of an era
The end of a sound
The birth of a memory
Forever around
Imagine a song
A story, a lover
Imagine a Christmas
When war is over
New life over sea
And games with the mind
With Rocket and Star men
And Fame of a kind

Just like starting over
And comeback the man
A night of recording
Dakota - a fan?
Multi news broadcasts
In sheer disbelief
A world heart broken
A world in grief
A legacy remains
The lingering taste
Imagine the world without..........
What a waste.

NHS

There's a terminal illness in the NHS
The futures pretty damn bleak I guess
It hardly comes as great surprise
Lack of funds and government lies
Disillusioned medics are lured away
No performance at the theatre today
They're overrun and understaffed
Organisation? They're having a laugh
Frustration, chaos all exists
We're dying to get on waiting lists
No beds for bodies waiting to mend
Dumped in a corridor for hours on end
Doctors and nurses all overworked
While admin responsibilities shirked
It's now the way the process goes
There's barely time to diagnose
Get in, get out, don't stick around
You'll only end up in the ground.
With promises broken and procedures ducked
All points to the fact that the systems f***ed
So help the profession from more distress
And stop making cuts to the NHS.

IT'S MY WORLD TOO

I see what I see, I hear what I hear
I live it my way, I play it by ear
Don't think it strange don't alter your speak
Don't think me different, but think me unique
My course is on track, by everyday actions
I won't digress, won't acknowledge distractions
I live my life fully, in my wonderful way
Have the best of all times and embrace everyday
I may come from left field, play with the form
Excel and confound, but this is the norm
Don't expect the expected, expect what you get
Accept what you see and you'll never regret
Happy to take and more so to give
Give love and that's all, then live and let live

It's my world too

MODERN LIFE

Is a house really ever a home
Or is home a state of mind
Abode a la mode
Where belongings are stowed
And memories are confined

In my semi detached relationship
Car I can't afford
A need to feed
A capitalist greed
Principals ignored

In my open plan penthouse life style
Hi- rise hedonism
Face in the crowds
Bed in the clouds
Antisocial socialism

In my bungalow life experience
One storey counts for all
Spin them a line
Wholesome, divine
Make it your curtain call

I AM

I'm the wine in your glass
I'm your male first class

I'm the bullet in your gun
I'm the cream in your bun

I'm the tonic in your gin
I'm the hob-nob in your tin

I'm the mate in your soul
I'm the toad in your hole

I'm the tone on your phone
I'm the flake in your cone

I'm the twinkle in your eye
I'm the meat in your pie

I'm the beans on your toast
I'm your full Sunday roast

I'm the sweet fruit in your jam
I'm the mint sauce on your lamb

I'm the bin to take your trash
I'm a sausage for your mash

I'm the walnut on your whirl
I'm the oyster round your pearl

I'm the cheese in your fondue
I'm the kick in your Vindaloo

I'm the singer of your ballad
I'm the dressing on your salad

I'm the powder in your keg
I'm the Mayo on your egg

I'm the alcohol in your liquors
I'm the big nuts in your snickers

I'm your hero, I'm your fool
I'm your multipurpose tool

I'm the rider on your pillion
I'm a linguist to your Brazilian

I'm your first teenage crush
I'm the one bird in your Bush

I'm the dock leaf for your nettles
I'm the bee around your petals

I'm your sneaky little fox
I'm the jack in your box.

I'm the star of your event
I'm the pole in your tent

I'm the pressure in your tyre
I'm the poker in your fire

I'm the strobe with your beat
I'm the probe in your meat

I'm the beating in your heart
I'm the rhubarb in your tart

I'm your donkey on the beach
I'm the juice in your peach

I'm the cuckoo in your nest
I'm the treasure on your chest

I'm a bather in your fountain
I'm a climber up your mountain

I'm your beer from Bavaria
I'm the balls in your play area

I'm the torpedo in your sea
I'm the boat docked in your quay

I'm the cure for your fever
I'm the log for your beaver

I'm the striker you'll never forget
I'm the ball in the back of your net

I'm your goalkeeper on the line
I'm your orange to suck at half time

I'm the hiker in your valley
I'm the cat up your back alley

I'm the guy you need to have some fun
If you want an innuendo I'll give you one

It'll take all this to make you see
I'm the one for you you're the one for me.

PERFECT DAY

See the break
From darkened skies
Morning calls
The sun to rise
Pierce the blinds
The rays shine through
Silvery light
Cascading you
On the streets
Bakers crafting
Early risers
Caffeine wafting
Fishing boats
Return from sea
Gulls will hover
Expectantly
Crystal waters
Ebbing calm
Golden beach
Swaying palms
Wispy clouds
Floating high
Decorate the
Clear blue sky
Take it in
Absorb the mood
Compose your own
Scenic etude

White sailed yacht
Skips the ocean
Gliding through
As in slow motion
See your footprints
In the sand
Take a step
Take a hand
Flattened pebbles
Bouncing, skimming
Striving, diving
Paddling, swimming
Hold that moment
Hold that thought
The days are magic
The nights are short
Stretching shadows
Sun descends
An orange sky
As daylight ends
New life starts
As sun goes down
Twinkling lights
Across the town
Room lights dim
Here to stay
Ends another
Perfect day

B & B

I love a Bed and Breakfast
But the rooms are so small
And the majority of those I know
Are contained within paper thin walls

And cavorting in the room next door
Hard at it all night and groaning
You hear every single syllable
Of dramatic, climatic moaning

The noisy rampant couple
Are so intense and so enthralled
All you can hear from next door
Is the rhythmic thud of slapping balls

There's nothing worse than hearing
Second hand sex in the air
From an over enthusiastic
Gymnastic newly-wed pair

It's depressing it's regressing
It's just completely wrong
Cos the young active buggers
Are lasting far too long

It makes you feel inadequate
And ego completely diminished
Because they're going at it like bunnies
Long after you would have finished

And what really makes it worse
And I'm sure that you'll agree
During all of this sexual vigorousness
I can't hear the bloody TV

All I can hear through the shenanigans
Is their mighty orgasmic wail
Which is spoiling my enjoyment
Of tonight's episode of Emmerdale

So to make me feel better in future
Amidst animated squeals and bed groans
I'll take with me to my hotel room
A pair of sound blocking headphones

IT'S OVER

She sits in bits
At the kitchen table
Unable
To get by
But only to cry
And in mother's tea
And sympathy
She sees
No sympathy
And the tea is cold
And the story's old
As time
And defined
By her mood
Ever changing
Disengaging
Her thoughts
Then are caught
In one moment
One gone moment
Her mind is torn
And the words won't form
To pull her through
And make her do
What she needs
Not just deeds

But commitment
To talking
Not walking away
Out of this
Desperation
To be rid of a face
In a place
She never asked to go
And never could show
All she needed
Was guidance
And advice
And more importantly
Love
To feel love
Real love
Not token love
Not taken love
Mistaken for love
It wasn't supposed to be
This way
That day
Her day
That special day
He walked away
And left her bereft
Of love of a kind
He took her heart
And took her mind

And as more tea
Goes cold
Memories
Grow old
And the tale
Grows stale
And again
She will say
Why wouldn't he stay
Couldn't you stay?
Not today
Things to do
No me and you
Any more
So now
You'll go
I know
Believe me
Even you
Will leave me
Too ...

SUMMER NIGHT

Summer night and music fills the air
Watch the sun go down without a care

I'm standing in the place
I always want to be
I'm landing in a space
I thought would never be

Summer night and laughter fills the air
I glance at you but try hard not to stare

I'm looking at the face
I always want to see
I'm thinking of the taste
Of lips so close to me

Summer night and dreaming fills the air
Wishes, hopes and thoughts all laying bare

I'm lying by the one
Your warmth against my skin
Pretense is all but gone
My life can now begin

Summer night and loving fills the air

LONDON BRIDGE HAS FALLEN.

And the land was struck with silence
And wheels began to turn
As London Bridge has fallen
And daily life's adjourned

A gathering of wishes
Envelopment of protection
A pouring out of media
A pouring of affection

A carefully played out theme
In everybody's story
Whether participant or observer
It's every person's glory

And commentators' comment
And bystanders stand by
And helplessness is abundant
As eyes stare at the sky

With bands and choirs in unison
And numbers beyond belief
United in a moment
Of indifference or grief

As people voice their feelings
With candour they won't hide
And children through innocent eyes
Take it in their stride

Just as any loved one leaves
A hole in whole appears
As family is fractured
In time of thoughts and tears

So, speak to me of life
And speak to me of learning
And speak of love and speak of peace
And wishes hopes and yearning

In grief is brought togetherness
In togetherness is hope
And hope will bring the strength we need
The strength to help us cope

London Bridge has fallen
As our own have gone before
Each loss must serve to ameliorate
Work through and not ignore

So, here's to futures different
Here's to cherished past
Here's to ones we all knew
With dedication unsurpassed

When looking to tomorrow
Where hope shines in the eyes
London Bridge has fallen
Let's watch a new bridge rise

QUESTIONS

Make a deal with me
And you got my soul
The devils in the detail
Just think of the goal
The word is in the tell tale
The answer in the whole
The world is my Oyster card
The benefits bank rolled
Make a deal with me
Take it all away
It's your turn to move
In a mysterious way
You're looking for the answer
Here's what you'll find
There's nothing in the wind
It's blowing your mind

INTERNATIONAL POETRY DAY

On international poetry day
I write something profound in rhyme
To astound, inform and impress
But I can't be arsed this time

AN OLD JOKE

The toilet attendant said to me
Its a bloody disgrace this place
People come here snorting coke
High and off their face
You get folks with drugs and illegal booze
Ruining their lives
I've even seen kids come in here
Carrying 8 inch knives
There's couples in cubicles having sex
It seems they just don't care
I tell you when someone just comes for a shit
It's like a breath of fresh air

TELL ME, IS THIS LOVE?

I'm checking my phone but there's nothing
I'll check again just to be sure
I'm thinking of some kind of paradox
Something devastatingly pure
And I'm feeling this pain like an emptiness
Like a loneliness, like a loss
Like a burden I carry for evermore
Like a gaping hole, like a cross
But as fast as it came it's gone
Clarity where all was blurred
And all it takes is a glance, a look
A message, a picture, a word
I remember a time when a style of life
Would send me running a mile
And the small things that drove me crazy
Do nothing but make me smile
There are flaws and imperfections
Well they are alright by me
I could now drown in what was my shallowness
I accept gladly all that I see
Now I'm checking my look in a mirror
Is it showing so clear on my face
As I grope for a hope of an answer
Does this face still have space in this place

If it's happiness why then the tears
From emotions not wanting to hide
As your face lights up the screen of my life
Brings that special feeling inside
Why is everything a reminder
Will the truth only come from above
I can't make any sense of these feelings, now
So please tell me, is this love ?

RHYTHM OF THE OCEAN

Cliffs bombarded
By waters of force
Blocking the way of
The tide on its course
The salty breakers
With crashing explosion
Play the one timeless tune that's
The rhythm of the ocean

Sculpted by time
And battering waves
Rock erosion,
Formation of caves
Inconceivable power
Overrules emotion
The mood is to swing to
The rhythm of the ocean

And fishermen delve
To make their living
The deep and the dark
Is so unforgiving
Through all of this
Marine commotion
The life drum beats to
The rhythm of the ocean

As ships bounce along
Like toys in a bath
Fighting the currents
To keep to their path
As phases of moon
Determine the motion
With winds orchestrating
The rhythm of the ocean

Disrespect of the sea
Is a misguided idea
Blind bravado
And hiding the fear
The thought of control
Is a foolish notion
Never underestimate
The rhythm of the ocean

TWO LITTLE LINES

It's a beautiful day
But it's with dismay
That I think of the places I could go
Quaint villages and towns
To have a stroll around
But two little lines say no

Wanna go to the pub
Get some beers and some grub
And relax in the suns warm glow
Chatting with mates
It all sounds great
But two little lines say no

Fish and chips
On seaside trips
Where coastal crisp winds blow
It seems ideal
But it's not, I feel
As two little lines say no

Walking in the Countryside
Someone special by my side
Always fun in sunshine or in snow
But it's not happening this week
As things are lookingpretty bleak
As two little lines say no

No shopping in the city
Much is the pity
No theatre for the latest show
Entertainment's at home
With the TV, alone
While two little lines say no

So there'll be no fun
It's a party for one
The futures pretty clear
It's so frustrating
To go on isolating
Till two little lines disappear

FRED DIBNAH

Oh Fred
We used to have a skyline
Till you dropped it from our eye line
And the chimneys towering high
Took the smoke into the sky
From the factories below
But there are none anymore
The areas all are cleared
As a new age now appears

Oh Fred
Steeplejack quite sublime
True character of our time
Reluctant celebrity
Working class integrity
A TV star, oh no
Fred's just the bloke next door
He may have fame but yet
What you see is what you get

And Fred
We saw you steaming by
With a twinkle in the eye
I'm certain that you knew
That we all cared for you
Scaling those crazy heights
With never a sign of fright
Yet even though we might care
You're a health and safety nightmare

And Fred
With your parping horn
A look somewhat forlorn
Smile and fag in gob
You turn to face the job
And when it's all complete
With rubble round your feet
You laugh and raise your hat
......'Did yer like that'

HEN PARTY

Like censored scenes
From magazines
Skin tight jeans
In stretch limousines
Pre-nup stress
In Wedding dress
Don't confess
That won't impress

It's a Silicone circus
All dressed for the purpose
The girls are on the town
And there's action going down

Learner plate
On champagne crate
No time to wait
Just hit it mate
Looking foxy
Fresh Botoxy
Selfies abundant
Morals redundant

Givin it a hellova lot
Getting high on what she's got
Necking back the jäger shots
These girls are smokin hot

Have some fun
Got some toys
Girls will be girls
Girls will be boys

Screams and shouts
And neat trout pouts
There's is no doubt
The girls are out

MOROCCAN SUNSET

A Moroccan sunset
A feeling closed
A haunted mind
A thought exposed

Through the smoky bar
Different rules apply
A piano played
As time goes by

And he plays tunes
For broken hearts
And people move
To safer parts

Now times are changing
The fear is real
And a passage out
Is the only deal

Of all the bars
What would be the chances
In all the places
To find where romance is

Here's looking at Paris
But can't ever be
Here's looking at true love
And setting it free

A midnight move
For a plight so chancy
A night of heartbreak
No flight of fancy

A Moroccan sun set
As day has passed
A forced au revoir
That couldn't last

OUR TIME

Through the gloom
Across the room
Aye aye to eye
Two passing by
A secret wink
Makes me think
It's our time

Giggles muffled
Exit shuffled
Knowing looks
Rooms are booked
One not used
Quite amused
In our time

Room with a view
A shower for two
Touching feet
Through silken sheets
Stolen kisses
That's why this is
Our time

The hours creep
No need of sleep
Forgetting past
Make this last
Loving flavour
Time to savour
In our time

Just one more day
And separate ways
Then in a while
Check out in style
How we made it
Wow we played it
In our time

THE POTATO (This is the food)

This is the veg
That we love and thank the lord above.
For making it nice
More adaptable than rice
The veg that will have you on edge
It'll swerve you
And un nerve you
And all the bad that you throw
It will still grow
Resolute this root
Despite the fight
Of potato blight,
The sight of this delight
That brought the world together forever
And whenever
We have to dash
For the mash
Be nippy
For the chippy
Cause a racket
For a jacket
Scream for creamed
Let's toast
The mighty roast
And we will grow yet
To embrace the croquette
And cease to look down
On the lowly hash brown

We give thanks
For this adaptable,
Edible vegetable so smart
Yet a work of art
Through Esther Rantzen being silly
With a spud shaped like a willy
So come together today and say ok
All is good we love a spud

For Kings and Queens
Were named it seems
After this vegetable glorious
Edward, Charlotte, Victoria
And king of all
The Jersey Royal

And who could ever
Endeavour
To risk life on the edge
With meat and no veg
So let's say as one
And sing as one
And praise as one
With love and care
The pomme de terre
That's spans the oceans
Remember - give love.....
And big portions.

Love the spud you're with.

WALK ME HOME

I met this girl at the youth club dance
We sat in a corner holding hands
I was quite obsessed but tried not to show her
I'd been madly in love since I heard she was a goer
She asked me if I'd walk her home
As she didn't want to walk alone
So I walked her back to her tenement flats
Which were securely guarded by a team of rats
I moved on in, got that first fumbled kiss
In a dirty elevator that stunk of piss
I ventured further with a glint in my eye
The lift was out of order and so was I
So I walked the 60 steps with youthful hope
Of the chance of a snog or a bit of a grope
I followed her in as she opened the door
I thought I might try for a little bit more
Then her dog wrapped its legs around my knee
I thought, hell the dogs getting more than me
So I kicked it off and held her hand
And thought about all that I'd planned
Just then her dad showed looking pretty mad
He said 'thanks for bringing her now bog off lad'
So I said goodnight and went down the 60 stairs
With a lack of action in my brand new flares
Three stairs to go and I hit a dog shit
Slid on the thing and went arse over tit

This wasn't going to be my night
As it ended with me half covered in shite
Sexual gratification was not to be
And I hung on intact to my virginity
So next time a girl asks me, I'll avoid the fuss
' Will you walk me home' 'No get a bloody bus !'

I KNEW A GIRL

I knew a girl
Whose smile
Brightened up a room
Whose zest for life
Was enviable
Whose mere presence
Was a bonus

I knew a girl
With strength
And determination
With so much love
To give
So much life
To live
Who deeply cared
With feelings shared

I knew a girl
With humour
In abundance
Who laughed
Infectiously
Cheekily
Wickedly
Often

I knew a girl
Who was a fighter
Driven and strong
Resilient
With belief
In what mattered

I knew a girl
Who you wanted to be with
Be seen with
Who turned company
Into good company
Into good times
Who knew life
And embraced it

I knew a girl
A popular girl
A beautiful girl
A funny girl
A girl I will miss
So very much
So VERY much

I knew a girl

THE INTERNET AGE

It's the internet age that's calling
There's a wind of change that's blowing
The standards of living are falling
Unemployment is the only thing growing

What's happening to our streets
What's happening to our towns
What happened to smile with a greeting
We're living in a land of frowns

There was industry all over
This was a land of opportunity
But factories shut and houses dropped
Destroyed what was our community?

There's a handful of bricked up churches
Pubs been shut down years
If beer and religion are your bag
I'm afraid it'll end in tears.

No Laundromat or Herbalist
The corner shops have pulled the shutter
The independent entrepreneur
Can be found face down in the gutter.

They tell us all is going fine
The faceless faces in the town hall
There's everything you want, they say
As long as what you want is sod all

I DON'T LIKE THE WEATHER

I don't like it too cold
I don't like it too hot
Don't like when it's breezy
Don't like when it's not
Don't like it too wet
Don't like it too dry
Don't like when dark clouds
Appear in the sky
Don't like it too cloudy
Don't like it too sunny
If I'm caught in the rain
I don't find it funny
Don't like it humid
Don't like it sticky
Don't drive when it's foggy
Find it too tricky
I don't like thunder
I don't like lightening
I find these weather
Conditions frightening
I moan and complain
Everyday of the weather
Why after this time
We can't get it together
Don't like all these changes
Different each day
So why the hell do I
Live in the UK

FESTIVAL FRIENDS

See the night
As sun descends
In a sea of lights
As daylight ends

Let's take a table for two
And dine and talk, of me and you
As the memories mesmerise
We turn old pages, raising eyes
Let's drink and think and reconnect
With stories that we recollect
Of youth and love and life and lust
And how we nearly, almost, just....
And let's move on and see the sights
And hear the music that delights
Within this crowd you're all I see
And this is where I want to be
Where all is good and all is fine
So cheers, we'll take in one more wine
And savour this, a magic time
And leave here with your hand in mine
A perfect night in warm July
'One day like this' will get me by
So look back and we had a blast
Although we can't relive the past
We can take strength in what this brings
A friendship that means everything

CHANGES

The skyline changing constantly
The city starts to rise
The old seems lost in shadow
Opinions polarised

Moving with demand
That's now the way it goes
Where classic architecture
And the modern juxtapose

Now non stop development
Progression has to happen
And turning our city
Into some kind of Manc-hatton

And on the streets shadows fall
Previous lifestyles masked
Forgetting, hiding, covering
What's left of the past

The streets our fathers built
And walked along each day
The factories that they slaved in
The visuals fade away

As generations move on
And change it has to come
Yesterday becomes insignificant
As developers have won

Cobbled streets and roads
Give way to faster needs
Businesses consolidate
Technology now breeds

And life is all convenient
But this comes at a cost
Our pubs our shops our high streets
Our communities all but lost

FIRE IN THE SKY

There is fire in the sky
As a nation stand by
And a world observes in shock
Of the horrors unfolding
Desperation withholding
Valiantly trying to block

Take flight as they might
As day turns to fright
Chaos surrounds on the street
And through smoke filled skies
That burn through the eyes
Attempting to beat a retreat

Dust clouds like a threat
Feature in silhouette
Obliterating visions of peace
Reality shrouded
Ideology crowded
No signs that the nightmare will cease

The children's marked faces
Tell a tale of the places
Dissected with rivers of tears
Tears we are seeing
Mothers holding and fleeing
From unprecedented fears

The children's marked faces
Tell a tale of the places
Dissected with rivers of tears
Tears we are seeing
Mothers holding and fleeing
From unprecedented fears

And a lonesome boy
Sees his favourite toy
Lie smouldering on the street
As he gently picks
Through piles of bricks
With his home beneath his feet

What meaning has home?
When you're roaming alone
In search of a piece of your past
Don't know where to start
As your life's blown apart
There's only slight hope left to grasp

And wanting and yearning
And climbing through burning
A hopeless and acrid thirst
A city of deference
Where hell seems a preference
A remnant of war at its worst

And smoke in the dark
Where once was a park
Where children's laughter was heard
Now no one ever goes
Where only death grows
And yesterdays dreams are absurd

A sky filled with flashes
The trees turn to ashes
And the birds no longer sing
And the sense in the air
Is the smell of despair
Anticipating the next sting

Resistance doomed to fail
Destruction will prevail
A shout and another's command
As they helplessly stare
At the horrors right there
As hundreds more fall on the land

More war is to blame
Just repeating the same
All the leaders have been miscast
Now mentalities strained
And nothing is gained
Will they never learn from the past?

WORDS

You look at me across the room
Those sparkling smiling eyes
With honesty and mischief
And a whole load of surprise

I look at you and see a beauty
Quite beyond compare
I smile, I know, I'm happy, that
There's something in the air

Something very special
A love that's only here
A love that conquers everything
Protects from harm and fear

Times we've spent together
Every minute loved and cared
And all those times wherever
The many words that we have shared

Words of learning and of teaching
Words of right and words of wrong
Words of other worldliness
Of where we all belong

Words that sometimes upset
Works that make us cry
Words that mean together forever
But never words that say goodbye

And I think back of those words
Happy memories shared gladly
Recalling the very first word
You ever said to me was daddy

OH I DO LIKE TO BE BESIDE THE....SEASIDE

On a sunny bank holiday the beaches are all full
They have their little picnics and stay till it goes dull
But they couldn't leave more rubbish there however
hard they tried
Oh I do like to be beside the......seaside

Their barbeque ashes are strewn across the beach
The seagulls will take all the waste food they can reach
And anything that's left there will be taken by the tide
Oh I do like to be beside the......seaside

There's empty cans of Coke and old papers galore
Cardboard cartons, plastic cups and even more
Everywhere you look there's pollution, you can't hide
Oh I do like to be beside the......seaside

There are fast food wrappers and other clutter here
Cigarette packets and condoms left under the pier
All kinds of everything that folks have chucked aside
Oh I do like to be beside the........seaside.

Seagulls choke on bottle tops, fish caught up in string
Wire netting ties up turtles and pretty much anything
Lots of other creatures that have washed ashore and died
Oh I do like to be beside the......seaside

So have a little think the next time that you come
Clear up all your rubbish and take it all home
And think about the consequence and have a bit of
pride
Because we all like to be beside the.....clean seaside

MUSIC WAS BETTER

Music was better
When I was a lad
Just look at all the
Stuff that we had
The Beatles, Dylan,
Elvis, Chuck Berry
T.Rex, Slade,
Bowie and Ferry
Not to mention The Pistols,
Clash, Undertones
We had Floyd, Jethro Tull,
And the Rolling Stones
Sabbath, Zeppelin
Kinks and the Who
Hardly comparable
With f***in Blue !
Little Mix and the Spice girls
Call themselves bands
Bands played instruments
With their mouths and their hands
And don't start me off
On Boy bands oh no
I'll tell you now
Where they can go
We'd real musicians
Like Winwood and Frampton

Hendrix, Page,
Beck and Clapton
And who is there now
To challenge the best
Beiber, Sam Smith
Kanye pissin West
There's Louis Capaldi
How he made the grade
And what will he do
When his looks start to fade
And back in the day
The stage clothes were top
Today there's more style
In a charity shop
No, music was better
When I was a lad
Even though I'm old now
I was there and I'm glad
So where will we be
When real music's gone
Oh yeah, I remember
Radio one

MIDSOMER MURDERS

Shot, stabbed, coshed, strangled
Drowned, clubbed, poisoned, mangled
Hit with bats and planks and girders
They drop like flies
On midsomer murders .....

And as the bag lady walks the street
There's menace waiting there to greet
In the shadows death unseen
A body lies on the village green

The cricket field holds some surprise
Captain with a stump between the eyes
In the woods there's no more rave
The DJ dumped in a shallow grave

In poor Midsomer the deadly power
5 dead bodies in the first half hour
Another body goes toppled off a bridge
And there's a couple hanging in the butchers fridge

The murder count is now starting to stack
Here comes Barnaby (that's Bergerac)
The village must have its own psychopath
The Vicars been found in an acid bath

Who is the murderer, nobody knows
It's not Mrs Petch who's been strangled with a hose
It's not Miss Cartwright the beautiful blonde
She's with the frogs at the bottom of the pond

At the blacksmiths forge a gruesome place
The blacksmith lies with an anvil on his face
Two minutes to go nearly time for bed
Bergerac gets his man - all the rest are dead

He finally got his murderer the only one to last
Pretty obvious really - the most famous of the cast
So just be warned there's nothing that is scarier
Than the comings and goings in the Midsomer area

Shot, stabbed, coshed, strangled
Drowned, clubbed, poisoned, mangled
Hit with bats and planks and girders
They drop like flies
On midsomer murders .....

They drop like flies
On midsomer murders .....

They drop like ....urgh

LOVER

Lover ....
All our time seems
Like a first date
All my feelings
You captivate
You're the reason
For my heart rate
You're my best friend
You're my soul mate

Lover.....
Lay by my side
With me tonight
Knowing you're safe
Knowing its right
Here in this place
You excite and delight
The fire that burns
In my heart you ignite

And lover....
I would never change a thing about you
Lover.....
I could never for a minute doubt you
Lover.....
I never want to spend a day without you

Lover.....
You're like no other
Lover.....
Never be another
Lover
Like you

I LOVE A CURRY

I love a curry
It's the spice of life
It's the food I see
It's the knees of the bee
It's the food that made me
Who I am
Tandoori chicken
Or Byriani Lamb
Praise the greatness
Of the vindaloo
I'd walk to the ends
Of the street for you
I'd like to try and
Start to form a
Relationship with my
Chicken korma

I'm overcome
With poppadum
I go batty
For a chapati
I'd sooner
Have a bhuna
I'm faulty
Without a balti
I'm getting keener
On a keema

I go crazy
For a jalfrezi
I'm on my ass
With no madras
My taste buds awash
With a rogan josh

Nothing could be grander
Than a wonderful passanda

The same goes too
With a saag aloo
More than a snack
A lentil dhansak
I get quite fickle
With raita and pickle
I'll always clamber
For a spicy samber
The bhajis and samosas
Are getting closer
A special treat that's a
Fiery dupiaza
I surely adore a
Fried fish pakora
Have with rice
But equally nice
Doesn't matter
Naan or paratha

Yes today make way
For a curry takeaway
Give thanks and pray
For the wonder of Bombay

So forget all of your troubles
Your fears or your worry
Cos the world revolves round
...............A bloody good curry

THE VALLEY

On the undulating valley slopes
With the bushes and skeletal trees
Old buildings sit in timeless glory
In the colourful autumn breeze

With a carpet of fallen leaves
To tread with a warming crunch
As the hungry squirrels do their work
Studiously gathering lunch

And the view overlooking the valley
With its buildings of beaten stone
Once cotton mills that lined the hills
From an age gone and weather blown

From mullions solid and ancient
Looking out over the tracks
With modern day restoration
Papering over the cracks

As you take the view on the valley top
Chimney stacks pierce the clouds
Last few remain from a bygone time
Still standing tall and proud

THE ROAD ARTIST

Got a hole in your road?
That the council won't repair
I know the very man
Artiste beyond compare

He's here on hand
With his tins of spray paint
With a piece of street art
Appropriate and quaint

Whenever he's needed
To get some attention
He'll paint around the pot holes
Things you shouldn't mention

If they don't repair the holes
To keep the balance
He'll draw attention
With a massive phallus

He blames it all on
The councils failure
Results in a display of
Road art genitalia

Doesn't do fancy murals
On bare brick walls
But show him a pothole and
He'll leave a cock n balls

A lifelike painted winkle
Adorning the road
Filling the pothole
With aerosol load

Where the roads have holes
In dilapidated parts
He'll embellish them
With ejaculatory art

Paints in hand as
Tools of the trade
Spray those holes
On a midnight raid

He's King of the road
When duty calls
The Cock of the North
The Belle of the balls

Indiscreet on the street
It's a bit of fun
He's quick and he's neat
He gets the job done

He may not quite have
The flair of banksy
But he gets roads fixed
Three cheers for 'wanksy'

HONOURS

Overlooked on the honours list again
Surely an almighty oversight
And after all the work that I've put in
An MBE at least should put it right

Not asking for a knighthood at this time
But recognition if it's all the same
An OBE or CBE are fine
I'd even happily accept a Dame

So come on Lizzie luv have a heart
I'm getting on a bit now you see
So don't leave it too late to make a start
Before all I end up with is an RIP.

TWO BOTTLE ARISTOTLE

There's one in every bar you call
The nobhead that thinks he knows it all
Can't take his drink and that's his downfall

With his pretentious turn of phrase
He brings upon a mild malaise
Your eyes will shortly start to glaze
They call him two bottle Aristotle

He's the multi lingual bore at the bar
With his irksome language seminar
Wish he'd just say au revoir

He'll give you his philosophies
His opinions and his prophesies
And much more other dross of his
Two bottle Aristotle

When he's had one drink he's on his box
Talking about science and the equinox
He's just a poundshop Brian Cox

A Primark Bryan Ferry
A melted Ben and Jerrys
A half baked Mary Berry
That's two bottle Aristotle

He's all pie in the sky
Like an approved school Stephen Fry
He's 'QI' without the 'I'

The 'I' with all the views
Opinions on the news
His schmooze will just bemuse
Choose to take a snooze
And avoid Two bottle Aristotle.

So if some light weight bends your ear
Then spoils the cheer and the atmosphere
Some mithering prick with a bottle of beer

While sitting through his pointless drone
You want to have a drink alone
You're wishing that he'll f*** off home
That's two bottle Aristotle

SEEMS TO ME

Seems to me ......
Times are changing over here
The truth has gone, cracks showing
Though the signs are crystal clear
Can't see where you're going
Addiction becomes way of life
To all others exclusion
All you get when you don't try
Disappointment and disillusion

Seems to me...
Good intentions may be ok
But broken promises not so
Like resolutions thrown away
At new year where to go
This is all pie in the sky
The relationship is strained
I'm competing with a lie
That can't ever be sustained

Seems to me ....
You don't know where to begin
This is illness born of stress
Fights an enemy within
Pour another shot of loneliness
It's yourself that is deceived
Acknowledgement is paramount
Pretence that's not believed
An illusion that cannot count

Seems to me .....
Only you can win this war
Consider why you do this
Consider who you do it for
And who you needlessly dismiss
Life is very precious
What future do you see
The love of someone special
Thrown away it seems to me

YOU'RE HAVING WHAT?

Crushed avocado on sour dough toast
Egg plant and kale on your Sunday roast
Tiny nouvelle cuisine stranded on a plate
Sausage, mash and 'jus' served on a slate
I think there's something odd and funny
About bulgar wheat with feta and honey
Poached quail eggs on asparagus spears
Pointlessly pushing culinary frontiers
Wilted samphire on Biltong cured beef
Yaks milk cheese wrapped in moringa leaf
This may all seem progressive and grand
But you're speaking a language I don't understand
Starbucks own Unicorn Frappuccino
Warm bruschetta with diced jalapeño
Pan seared halibut with triple cooked chips
Guacamole, tzatziki and ginger soy dips
You may think it's classy and posh
What the hell's the point of butternut squash
The menus no longer up to par
This time you've gone a little too far
Flash griddled line caught Arctic char
Oh what a pretentious tosser you are

LEARN TO FLY

Learn to fly
Out of the black
In the evening sky

Learn to see
Through the mist
Where the truth will be

Learn to walk
Away from pessimism
And negative talk

Learn to live
Without anomalies
And snags that won't give

Learn to think
Positive thoughts
Won't let you sink

Learn to try
To ignore hassles
That pass you by

Learn to cope
And change pitfalls
To highs of hope

Learn to take actions
To help ignore
Harmful distractions

Learn to be true
To be honest
To be you

I FORGOT TO TELL YOU

Hi, how you doing
just thought I'd ring you
hope you're ok
I've been thinking a lot
since you left
the other day
it was the right thing
even though I didn't want to
you were right
I know now
I'm sure of it

I forgot to tell you
how much fun I'd had
when we were together
do you remember that weekend
you know the one
when we first
well, you know

I forgot to tell you
remember Carols party
in Preston last year
well I still have the photos
oh they were funny
maybe I'll drop them off
we really did have some great times
didn't we

I forgot to tell you
I got that CD
from the band we saw
in Manchester
at that last night out
we had
together

I forgot to tell you
I may be moving soon
dunno where, just moving
I'll let you know
if you're interested
it doesn't matter

I forgot to tell you
I was out with the lads
on Tuesday
just having a brilliant time
got really drunk
you know me
really had a laugh
with the lads
like it should be
who needs girls eh
ha ha, only kidding

I forgot to tell you
I think I've got that new job
it's not much but
well, just thought I'd say
if you want, maybe
when you get this message
you could ring me back
only if you want
it's not that important
oh by the way
I forgot to tell you
So many times
I forgot to tell you

I love you......

MY 1970s

Space hopper, Raleigh chopper
Action man, Desperate Dan
Pea Shooters, running scooters
Corner shops, Top of the pops
School bus, Eleven plus
Fashion shirts, Miniskirts
Wide Flares, no cares
Wine gums, super mums
Fruit jubblys, Bazooka Joe bubblys
Bernie Inns, Red rum wins
Radiogram, Robertson's jam
Daily Star, Wimpy bar
Trim phone, Rag and bone
Scuffed knees, Philly cheese
Feather cut, Pizza Hut
Lads mag, E type Jag
Mayfair, Marie Claire
Grandstand, Promised land
Holiday Camp, lava lamp
Ford Capri, Queen's jubilee
Glam rock, speaking clock
Blue nun, cap gun
Tea cosy, Mateus Rose
Party line, moonshine
Wilson, Heath, Corned beef
Workers Strikes, Yamaha bikes
Three day week, futures bleak

Watergate, in a state
Moon exploration, Decimalisation
Summer of 76 Sticklebricks
Hot pants, Brian Cant
Robin Day, Maggie May
UDA, IRA,
TUC, BBC
Red phone box, closing docks
Tabloid sins, piled up bins
Scooby doo, Dr Who
Colour TV, Simon Dee
Uncle Joe's, So it goes
Crown Court, World of Sport
Pebble mill Grange Hill
Super trooper, Tommy Cooper
Wacky races, Bobby's braces
Georgie Best, Whistle Test
Mark Spitz, Manchester Ritz
Free trade hall, Band on the wall
Bolton Palais, Mohammad Ali
Royal brothers, Frank and The Mothers
Stirling Moss, Albatross
Man Alive, Derek and Clive
Kevin Keegan, Jack Regan
Bambi, Dumbo, Lieutenant Columbo
Grease, Jaws, Star Wars
Live and let die, American pie
Farmers arms, Teenage charms
Underage booze, platform shoes.

Bolton college, New found knowledge
Dylan's words, snoggin 'birds'
T Rex, fumbly sex
School leavers, party fever
Mighty Reds
Cool threads
Skinheads
Blockheads
Dreads
Garlic bread,
Bunk beds
Watneys Red
The King is dead!
'Nuff said

COMMUTING

The seats are now taken with all on their missions
Commuting in ritualistic conditions
And stare through the windows take in all that passes
Regulated and segregated by classes
Old factory chimneys poke holes in the sky
Tenement blocks are as one passing by
Timeless architecture blends with the new
A juxtaposition contained in the view
Mindless sub culture paper over the cracks
Musical soundscape conceived on the tracks
Comforting rhythm familiar scales
Percussive, intrinsic pounding the rails
And city life drifts off, left far behind
As grey turns to green transformation aligned
And fields pass like life through snapshots of time
Like a come to life Lowry indicative, sublime
Rivers and streams flow past, cutting through land
Images flash by, appear bland to grand
Then the rhythm slows down, the green back to grey
Travellers regimentally making their way
As the crowds become lines splitting through stations
And the story has ended at their destinations.

THE CURSE OF 'STRICTLY'

We all know the curse
Of strictly come dancing
Getting up close
Clandestine romancing
Eyes are glued
Across the nation
For that secret smile
And a bit of flirtation
Remember it always
Takes two to Tango
Getting all horny
In the throws of a Fandango
Hit the floor with
A simple Bossa nova
Behind closed door
For a quick leg over
Erotic Rumba
Rough and tumble
In the Samba
Stumble a fumble
Up close Salsa
In it for a little
Chance of a bit of
Slap and tickle
Don't give no Jive
Just expectation
A Quickstep in
The right direction

Up close and personal
La de da
Everyone likes a bit of
Cha cha cha
Do the Bop
Do the Stroll
Have a bit of Rock
And have a little roll
Get some Zumba and
Waltz my way
Make a pass
Make a Pasodoble
Getting hot now
Sweat on sweat
Eye to aye aye
In the Minuet
Things are getting racy
Things are getting worse
Welcome one and all
To the strictly curse

WRESTLING HERO

The Albert halls in Bolton
Excitement all around
A dream came true for this kid
The wrestling had come to town
And all the names were there
We'd seen on our TV
Giant Haystacks and Big Daddy
But it was Kendo Nagasaki for me
The king of the ring was Kendo
A hero to this young lad
With flamboyant style he had it all
He was tops, he was ace, he was bad
The mystery man of grappling
A superman of the sport
A whirlwind of wrestling excellence
Could cause storms in any port
As the ladies on the front row
Flailed handbags from their seats
While the greatest masked attraction
Performed his stylish feats
Strutting the ring imperiously
Amid boos and chants and jeers
The referees appeals and warnings
Fall on his covered ears

With specialist moves his agenda
Is to see off opponents with style
They'll have their little moments
But it's only for a while
He bounds back into action
With seconds left to spare
A kamikaze rollover
The arms are in the air
The bell has gone its finished
Our hero wins the bout
And the spectacle is over
And all the crowd file out.
So we head off for the bus stop
And reflect on our great day
And we all stand and watch in awe
As a masked man drives away

With the man himself Kendo Nagasaki (Peter Thornley)
in 2022. That kids hero is now a friend!

MIDDLE AGED ANARCHY

I'm not having a dry September
I'm not growing a moustache in November
I'm not stopping smoking
You've gotta be joking
I'm not having a meat free December

Don't tell me to upgrade my phone
Or try to give me a loan
I never did buy
Any PPI
I have a sound mind of my own.

I'll have pancakes on a Sunday
Go to church on Monday
I'll celebrate valentine
On February twenty nine
And have a summer holiday in Mumbai

I don't want to change my utilities
I'm happy with current facilities
So stuff your Meerkat
Then Go compare that
Before we begin the hostilities

I'm not one for doing as I'm told
I'll gladly swear blind hot is cold
I don't listen to voices
I make my own choices
It's a privilege of getting old

I eat after eights at ten to
I never do things when I'm meant to
If a meeting starts at 11
I'll be there at 11.07
I'll not have anyone tell me when to

I'll eat chocolate eggs at Christmas
Black peas on the 4th of July
Roast turkey and trimmings
When everyone's slimming
Oh how anarchic am I.

HELP ME

Help me out of this darkness
This unnatural darkness that takes me over
These feelings that are unaccountable,
unfathomable, but still there
Hanging like a heavy cloud,
like a weight of misery,
like chains holding me back

Help me see through this darkness
This irrational yet inevitable state of mind,
state of being,
state of attitude.
Where there is need for reassurance
Where there's more tunnel at the end of the light,

Help me cast away the darkness
that haunts my being,
that crushes my ambition,
that laughs in my face,
The darkness of hopelessness.

Help me shake off this darkness,
this snapshot of a time,
this series of blurred images,
these deeply embedded mental wounds

Help me on the other side of darkness
To feed on hope and anticipation
Thrive on the nourishment of company,
Be rid of the scars within that came from loved ones
and learn to live and trust again

Help me shine a light into the darkness
where the shaded is uncovered
Shine a light of clarity
to make the ambiguous clear,
the duplicitous ingenuous
the mendacious honest,
that I may believe what I see
and have no fear

If you help me

2020 VISION

It's now been many months
Since our lives were turned around
With sufferings and hardship
Yet strength we somehow found
With great determination
In the face of all that came
Resilience of a nation
Understating the waiting game
And all the hurt thrown at us
Despite all this came through
Because togetherness matters
We're Brits it's what we do.

What a year of fears
Of heartbreak, of tears
Of hardships unspoken
Of families broken
Of sorrow and stress
Faith put to the test
And boundaries crossed
At a cost
And those that we lost
Those that we lost

But the time still looked bleak
As the days turned to weeks
Feeling entombed
We sat there in a room

Conversing through zoom
Reflecting the gloom
All getting too much
With no physical touch
With worry and uncertainty
We battle through determinedly
And like brothers
Helped each other
Recover and discover
Community
Standing in unity
Yet time went by
And beer pumps ran dry
Shops opened and closed
Livelihoods disposed
People neglected
Unprotected, rejected
But all were valid
We endured and we rallied
With time to spare for
Those we care for
Hope and therefore
Say a prayer for
Those with so much to lose
That minds were confused
Feeling distraught
Those feelings we fought
But still came dark thoughts

Of where now to go
What did we know
For answers we groped
And while everyone hoped
Not everyone coped
Not everyone coped

As the virus stormed
We stood firm and conformed
And although frustrated
Aggravated, deflated
We stayed safe, we isolated
Toeing the line
Biding our time
While doctors and nurses
Defied Covid's curses
And stoically
Heroically
They gave time
With devotion sublime
And a mountain to climb
Their lives on the line
We were all involved
And with great resolve
We stood tall and proud
We all spoke loud
In applause
Of the cause

Of our appreciation
From all the nation
And as time then rolled on
And some battles were won
Science was quite a friend
The tunnel has light at the end
And as vaccines were made
Solidarity conveyed
Optimism displayed
And we hoped and we prayed
Through a time so fateful
Now we can be grateful
To be able to say
We are here today
Me and you
We've come through
We've come through

ALL I NEED

I can live without cigarettes
Get high without cocaine
I don't wanna marijuana
Won't try no heroin
I don't need rum or whisky
To wake my enthusiasm
I can get by very nicely thanks
With a cocktail of beer and sarcasm

I don't want artificial uppers
To get me on a meaningful high
It's just the simple things in life
Like you, that gets me by
The thrust of endless substances
Like a narcotic neoplasm
Are wasted on this guy who just wants
Some beer and sarcasm

Beer and sarcasm my raison d'être
It's all that I want to be
I rarely say anything that I regret
Just call it repartee
My tone comes from a good place
No one here's at fault
Don't take offence at what I say
Just take with a pinch of assault

Beer and sarcasm my conversation
I'm not impressed with your views
Of happenings all across the nation
Don't bring me your mind numbing news
Don't use me to discuss and expound off
I don't do small talk and chat
You'll sulk when I start to sound off
Your tediousness draws me to that

Beer and sarcasm a match made in heaven
At home in my very own local
It's the natural environment
For getting pissed and quite vocal
The time and place for discussion
For putting the world to rights
The perfect place for arguments
Abusive behaviour and fights

And all of them right of course
Their opinions kindly shared
I'd love to debate the matters all night
If I even fuckin cared
The gap between people's politics
Seems an unbridgeable chasm
So I'll leave them to their particular ways
And stick with my beer and sarcasm

POUNDSHOP

Every town's treat
On the main shopping street
The mighty poundshop
To greet the elite

It's the latest thing
Be sure to bring
A quid to spend
Where the pound is king

Clever shopping pays
So change your ways
Buy electrical items
That work for days

All new shopping
There's no stopping
Head down now for
Pound shop hopping

Pound shop
Pound shop
Shop like you can't stop
Pound shop
Pound shop
Shop till you drop

It's so jolly
It's all folly
Grab the crap
And fill your trolley

Have a good look round
Bargains to be found
You don't ask the prices
Everything's a pound

Pound goods galore
From ceiling to floor
Get some tat
Then get some more

Pound shop
Pound shop
Shop like you can't stop
Pound shop
Pound shop
Shop till you drop

Danny Dyers memoirs
T-Cut for shiny cars
4 pack of mars bars
Best value by far

A dodgy watch from china
There's really nothing finer
It's all there for a pound
But it's hardly designer

Don't make an offer
Don't make a bid
Take what you like
The price is a quid

If you need a takeaway
Amid all this fakery
Then pop in next door
To the great pound bakery

Pound shop
Pound shop
Shop like you can't stop
Pound shop
Pound shop
Shop till you drop

A bell for a bike
A map for a hike
Ideal gifts
For people you don't like

Go and feed
Your pound shop greed
And get some shit
That you don't need

When a bargain you chance on
Go and get your hands on
Grab as many as you can
Cos when it's gone it's gone

Pound shop
Pound shop
Shop like you can't stop
Come on now chop chop
Think of the backdrop
The tip top work shop
The children in the sweat shop
To fully stock your pound shop
So shop till you drop

WILLY?

The contents of a man's pants
Though not particularly pretty
That fascinate and amuse
Are the subjects of this little ditty
It's easy to remember the name
No way could you make a mistake
There's a million different words
For the mercurial trouser snake

They call em nobs and dicks and cocks
And raging, raving jack in the box
Ding dong,wanger, doinker
Wing wang, bong and plonker
A guaranteed joybringer
The bald headed yoghurt slinger
The private pocket monster
The todger, the lairy loin lodger
The love measure to treasure
The pump of perfect pleasure
Trouser arouser triceratops
The leaping, weeping Cyclops
The bringer of wham bam
The salty battering ham
The family builder
The long dong silver
The sex six shooter
The rootin tooter

The burrowing worm
The pistol of sperm
The magic wand, the pecker
The probing place checker
The joystick, the weenie, the winkle
The organ, the chopper, the tinkle
The member, the tool, the root
The sausage, the mighty pink flute
The hosepipe, the python, the dong
The pocket rocket, the schlong
The racy tasty frankfurter
The throbbing main vein squirter
The big beef bayonet, the king
The hanging middle leg, the dingaling
Lengthy love muscle, pork dagger
Terminator, throat gagger
The plug, the thug, the conceiver
The mighty beaver cleaver

So many different names
I'm sure I've not said them all
It really is far too much fuss
About something that's so small

THESE ARE THE SIGNS OF THE TIMES

Faces stuck to mobile phones
Congregating in wifi zones
A configuration of bland ring tones
These are the signs of the times

Retail, the writings on the wall
Corner shops, we've lost em all
Shuttered fronts on the shopping mall
These are the signs of the times

Real Pubs close down such a shame
Fancy wine bars the name of the game
Eateries with unpronounceable names
These are the signs of the times

Vapes now used in every place
Pumping aromas in my face
I'd like to reciprocate with mace
These are the signs of the times

Lips by surgery for that special pout
Piercing in places we don't talk about
Botox should take away any self doubt
These are the signs of the times

Shopping now all done on line
Don't get choice you don't have time
Didn't have grapefruit so we sent you lime
These are the signs of the times

Pop music's not got the style it had
Most of its crap now, just a tad
I know, I'm sounding like me dad
These are the signs of the times

TV pampers to the baser factions
A weary world needs a hi brow distraction
But they settle for love island and naked attraction
These are the signs of the times

Cookery programmes on TV every night
But there's no way to taste it so that can't be right
For all we know everything tastes shite
These are the signs of the times

The skies infested with bloody drones
Non stop selfies from mobile phones
Cameras all over you're never alone
These are the signs of the times

Specialist diets now everywhere
Check those allergens, and take good care
Dinner can kill you so do beware
These are the signs of the times

Doctor's surgeries no longer cope
Ask for appointment but there's no hope
Easier to get an audience with the pope
These are the signs of the times

Churches turned into luxury flats
21st century habitats
Swallowed up by ponsy yuppie twats
These are the signs of the times

If you come to this country for a bit of a gander
And you think that nothing could be grander
Watch out or they'll send you to Rwanda
These are the signs of the times

The NHS is on the rocks
First Covid 19 now monkey pox
It's like someone's re-opened Pandora's box
These are the signs of the times

Can't afford petrol and nor can you
Utility bills gone through the roof too
I'm not much enjoying 2022
These are the signs of the times

At the end of 2021 I sadly lost my mother.
These final three poems were written at that time for her.
They are probably the only poems in this book
that she didn't get to read.

THERE'S A HOLE IN MY LIFE

There's a hole
In my life
Where unconditional love
Used to reside
Emptiness I feel
A loss that shouts out
In a way
I can't hide

And that which
Was always there,
Always available,
Whether needed or not
Is now a memory
A past guide,
A shoulder,
That I've no longer got

And I now feel
Insecurity
Vulnerability
Expended
And the reality
Is a realisation
Of how much
I depended

And grief shouldn't be
Confused with self pity
It manifests
In many ways
The time has come
To move on
Take new responsibilities
And take my place

I need to remember
That the past was good
And therefore
Not to be sad
Don't have pain
For what I lost
But joy and thanks
For what I had

WHO?

Who do I tell my news to
Who silver lines all my clouds
Who will patiently be there all day
Who will smile and always be proud

Who do I confide in
Share my inner most thoughts
Who advises calmly
When all my problems are brought

Who will humour my whims
From that non judgmental place
Who will listen to all my dreams
With always a loving embrace

Who do I turn to now
Who can I look to, to care
Because where the answers laid
There now sits an empty chair

THE LAST TRIP

Cast to the winds
Over sands remembered
Of holiday games
And times in Septembers
Bonding with friends
And families together
Braving the elements
In autumnal weather
A lifetime in seconds
Recount by relations
Of times so well lived
Passed to new generations
So fly 'cross the bay
A spirit goes free
Blend into horizon
Glide over the sea
And leave in deep thought
That last ending rhyme
A poetic goodbye
This one final time

TESTIMONIALS & REVIEWS

"A great read, nostalgic, funny and much more"

Pete Turner (musician songwriter Elbow)

Positively bridling with genuine humour, empathy, pathos and inclusivity, Steven P. Taylor hits home hard with tales that need hearing about joy, grief and the experience of life – not just ours, but those which have shaped and secured generations. A consummate poet, whose poems are at home on the page and the stage.
Paul Neads, (Flapjack Press)

'marvellously mischievous and thought provoking' - **The Met Arts centre Bury.**

Steven. P Taylor's poetry is a heady mix of the humorous , the divine and the deep , composed in an imaginative synthesis of vernacular and the sacred with a combination of wit and wonder …..
Tom Hingley (singer songwriter, Inspiral Carpets)

'Brilliant poet …..**Phil Walker (comedian)**

'Really great poetry'
George Borowski (Musician / songwriter)

From time to time, if we're lucky, we get to meet folk who have a gift, a rare talent of connection. They can make things, write, draw, sing, play, sculpt - and with it they communicate on a level which can change the way you think, make you see things in a different way, see the funny and tragic in the everyday.

When however, these people are genuinely self-effacing and work with a passion that is totally unconnected to their ego, then seeing them work is a pleasure in itself. When Steven took to the stage of the Bury Met in his first theatre show since lockdown in Feb 2022, the warmth from the crowd reflected all of these things. He's got the gift.......

Andy Hollingworth (celeb photographer and comedy fan)

 Arresting engaging poetic verse laced with class A Northern humour…

Vinny Peculiar (musician, songwriter, poet)

Steven is an entertaining and clever rhymer who keeps an audience involved and on their toes.

Dave Morgan ('live from worktown')

As promised, here are some of the 'Bury Met' reviews from the public, that were posted on social media

Emma Felicity
An amazing night, great mixture of serious/ sad/ and could've rolled off my chair laughing. ◉◉ can't wait for your next one x

Jane Kelly
I loved every minute. Thank you for a great night ◉xx

Karen Dodgson
It was a fantastic evening, we really enjoyed it. Well done Steve x

Lynn Nichols
Amazing evening, every emotion possible. You certainly know how to touch people's hearts.
See you same time next year ◉

Hazel Teal
what a fantastic night we had. You are amazing - tears of laughter and tears of sadness awesome humour and wit. Thank you xx

Pam Ashton
It was a fab evening SPT

Horace Dogson
Jolly good show. Furrily enjoyed it.

Denise Lucas
Superb

Carl Smith
Yet another great night Steve. The Caverns loss was our gain. But home turf is always best. Keep it up

Amanda Deane
You were fab last night!! Haven't laughed that much in months

Georgia Leigh Taylor
You were so good I actually can't say it enough!!

Michele Richardson
Brilliant night. You should be proud of yourself you get better each time

Janet Rubanik
Awesome!
Wonderful evening. My friends and I loved it.

Linda Jennings
Brilliant show

Kathy Enfield
It was a brilliant evening.

Paul Jones
Great night

Cerys Ward
Fantastic night

Keith Campbell
Excellent night

Thank you all, whether buying my books or coming to my shows, spreading the word, commenting and sharing social media posts or just saying nice encouraging things.
What a lovely group of people you are, I'm very lucky.

Steven xx

Dedicated to the memory
of
Jack and Jean Taylor